THE PICTURE
LIFE OF
BILL COSBY

THE PICTURE LIFE OF
BILL COSBY
BY BARBARA JOHNSTON ADAMS

A GROLIER COMPANY

FRANKLIN WATTS 1986
NEW YORK LONDON TORONTO SYDNEY

The quotation on page 44 is from Jane Hall,
People magazine, December 10, 1984
and is used by permission.

The quotation on page 47 from *You Are
Somebody Special* is used by permission. (*You
Are Somebody Special* is part of a program called
Skills for Living, designed and published by The
Quest National Center, 6655 Sharon Woods
Boulevard, Columbus, Ohio.)

Cover photograph courtesy of Archive Pictures © Michael O'Brien

Photographs courtesy of: AP/Wide World:
pp. 2, 6, 13, 14, 18, 21, 22, 24, 29, 30, 33, 34, 38,
41, 42, 45, 46; Ted Polumbaum, People Weekly
© 1977 Time, Inc.: pp. 10, 26; UPI/Bettmann
Newsphotos: p. 17; Children's
Television Workshop: p. 37.

R. L. 3.6 Spache Revised Formula

Library of Congress Cataloging in Publication Data
Adams, Barbara Johnston.

Includes index.
Summary: Follows the life and career of the popular
black entertainer, from his childhood in Philadelphia
to his success as a comedian and actor.
1. Cosby, Bill, 1937—Juvenile literature.
2. Entertainers—United States—Biography—Juvenile
literature. 3. Comedians—United States—Biography
Juvenile literature. [1. Cosby, Bill, 1937—
2. Comedians. 3. Entertainers. 4. Afro-Americans—
Biography] I. Title.
PN2287.C632A64 1986   792.7′028′0924 [B] [92] 85-29487
ISBN 0-531-10168-1

TO LARRY AND HILARY
WITH LOVE

I would like to thank the staff members of the
Reston Regional Library, Reston, Virginia, for
their continued enthusiastic support of my
research. In addition, special thanks go to Shana
Conway, Nikki McKinney, Sarah Connerley, John
Ignosh, Jessica Redlin, and my daughter, Hilary Adams.
My editor, Adriane Ruggiero, helped and encouraged
me throughout.

Each week all over America over 30 million people turn on their television sets to watch "The Cosby Show." Children and adults laugh at the things that happen to the show's star, Bill Cosby, and to his TV family of a wife and five children. "How did they find out what's happening in my house?" many viewers think as they watch.

And that's exactly what Bill Cosby wants. He created the show because, in real life, he *has* five children. Several years ago he didn't like the television programs they were watching. The programs often showed ugliness and violence. People on TV never seemed to be having a good time. Most importantly, Bill Cosby knew there was no television show that showed a loving black family.

A scene from "The Cosby Show."
Cliff (Bill Cosby) gives Vanessa
(Tempestt Bledsoe) some
advice on playing the clarinet
after he discovers she
can't play a note and her recital
is in three days.

(7)

So he decided to have a series of his own about the Huxtable family. A doctor father and lawyer mother are shown as a successful couple who care very much about one another and about their children. This is the first time a regular TV show has shown a black family this way.

But people watching forget that the Huxtable family is black. The family could be any family living down the block or across the street. All that matters is that the Huxtables and their children are funny and loving and caring. They laugh with one another over the little ups and downs of life. Through laughter, the family is able to teach something, too.

One of the programs shows what happens when a goldfish dies. The fish belongs to the family's youngest daughter, Rudy. At first some family members feel foolish getting dressed in their good clothes for a goldfish's funeral. And the audience chuckles when the family stands in the bathroom ready to bury the fish by flushing it down the toilet. But then mother, father, sisters, and brother show their understanding of Rudy's sad feelings about the death of her pet.

Viewers of the show are eager to express how they feel. One child in Virginia said, "I like the way the kids on the program are like real-life brothers and sisters because they argue and tease each other."

A great success, "The Cosby Show" was the number-one-rated series on television its first season on the air.

Bill Cosby's childhood was very different from that acted out by the children on his TV series. William Henry Cosby, Jr., was born in 1937 in Philadelphia, Pennsylvania. His family and others living nearby were poor and sometimes did not have enough to eat. Anna, Bill's mother, worked as a housemaid. Since his father was in the navy he was away from home for months at a time.

Mrs. Anna Cosby,
Bill's mother

Bill was the oldest of three brothers (a fourth brother died while still a child) and Anna depended on him for help while his father was not home. After school he cooked (his specialties were waffles and popcorn), looked after his brothers, and did some cleaning. When she had time, Anna read to Bill from books written by Mark Twain, an American author famous for his stories of mischievous boys like Tom Sawyer and Huckleberry Finn. Bill especially enjoyed these tales. Anna also read from the Bible.

Unlike some of the neighborhood children, Bill stayed out of serious trouble because he didn't want to disappoint his mother.

In 1968 Bill visited the Philadelphia neighborhood where he grew up

In elementary school he was known as a "clown." Bill liked making people laugh, and he took part in school plays. He was good at sports, especially baseball and track. In the classroom, however, he was not a star and his report cards showed poor marks.

By the time Bill was in high school he had become an excellent athlete and was captain of the football team. Although he was smart, Bill just couldn't keep his mind on his studies. Sports and just plain "horsing around" were his main interests. He had to repeat tenth grade and finally dropped out of school.

Bill Cosby and actor Will Geer
in a scene from his 1970 TV show,
"The Bill Cosby Show"

With little education it was difficult finding challenging work. One poorly paid, uninteresting job followed another. Eventually Bill decided to join the navy.

Four years in the navy were a turning point in Bill's life. He found out he wanted to do something that gave him a sense of satisfaction. He also wanted to earn good pay so his mother wouldn't have to work.

While he was still in the navy, Bill took courses and received his high school diploma. Then he decided to go to college. In 1961, when he was 23, Temple University in Philadelphia offered him an athletic scholarship.

Bill Cosby played football at Temple University in the early 1960s. Here, he holds a picture of himself after being inducted into the Temple Hall of Fame.

At Temple, Bill did well both as a student and as an athlete. For a time he thought he would be a gym teacher. But he had second thoughts after finding a part-time job.

As a bartender at a night club in Philadelphia, Bill couldn't resist joking with the customers. The owner saw that the customers enjoyed the jokes and offered to hire him as a comedian. When Bill accepted he unknowingly took a step into his future.

Word spread about the new comic's talents. In his act he used stories that had their roots in his childhood. Experiences with his friends or memories of school days came together in his imagination. One of the characters he created was the black inner-city boy named Fat Albert, whose favorite remark is, "Hey, hey, hey!"

Fat Albert is one of Bill Cosby's
most well-known characters. Here,
the comedian is shown on his TV show
"Fat Albert and the Cosby Kids."

When Bill told a story he moved the features of his face around as though they were made of rubber. He also added sounds that made what he was saying even funnier.

Throughout Bill's career he has kept on making funny faces and noises. He has imitated his brother Russell's laugh by making *arp*, *arp*, *arp* sounds that remind audiences of seals in the zoo at feeding time. While talking about dogs he has pointed out that if a Saint Bernard tries to bark twice in a row he'll get so exhausted he'll go *woof—arragh* and die of a heart attack.

The many faces of Bill Cosby

Other night clubs offered him jobs; he was invited to appear on TV. Bill was in a difficult spot. On the one hand he liked sports and was proud he was doing well in college. On the other hand he knew he had a chance to break into show business. But what a risky business it is! Only a few comedians ever become top entertainers.

Nevertheless, Bill knew he'd never be satisfied unless he tried. So he left Temple University and began appearing before larger audiences in night clubs like the Hungry I in San Francisco and Basin Street East and the Bitter End in New York City.

Bill Cosby, early in
his acting career

He decided that in his comic routines he would concentrate on the experiences we have in common instead of the differences that can pull us apart. He stopped using humor based on people's skin color. Instead, he found the funny side of everyday events.

During the 1960s the risk Bill had taken in going into show business paid off. In addition to his night club act, he made records. *I Started Out as a Child*, *Why Is There Air?*, *Bill Cosby Is a Very Funny Fellow—Right!* and *Wonderfulness* were some of the titles. Through his records and live performances he was becoming famous. Over the years his records would win eight Grammy awards. Grammys are the top honors given by the recording industry and are similar to the Oscars for movies and the Emmy awards for television.

Bill during the taping of a television show in the United Nations General Assembly, 1970

In 1964 Bill took another important step when he married Camille Hanks. Camille was a 19-year-old student at the University of Maryland when Bill met her. They knew very soon that they wanted to marry. Camille's parents, however, were not pleased when they found out how Bill earned his living. They worried that he would not be able to give their daughter the kind of life they hoped she would have. But Camille and Bill went ahead and married. More than 20 years later their marriage is still a strong and happy one.

Camille Cosby,
Bill's wife

Today, the Cosbys have four daughters —Erika, Erinn, Ensa, and Evin, and one son, Ennis. Bill and Camille decided to give all their children names beginning with "E" because, as Bill says. "It's a way of reminding them each day throughout their lives that 'E' stands for excellence." The Cosbys always have expected a great deal from their children, but they also give them a home filled with love and respect.

Bill with his two eldest daughters, Erika (behind her father) and Erinn (leaning on his shoulder)

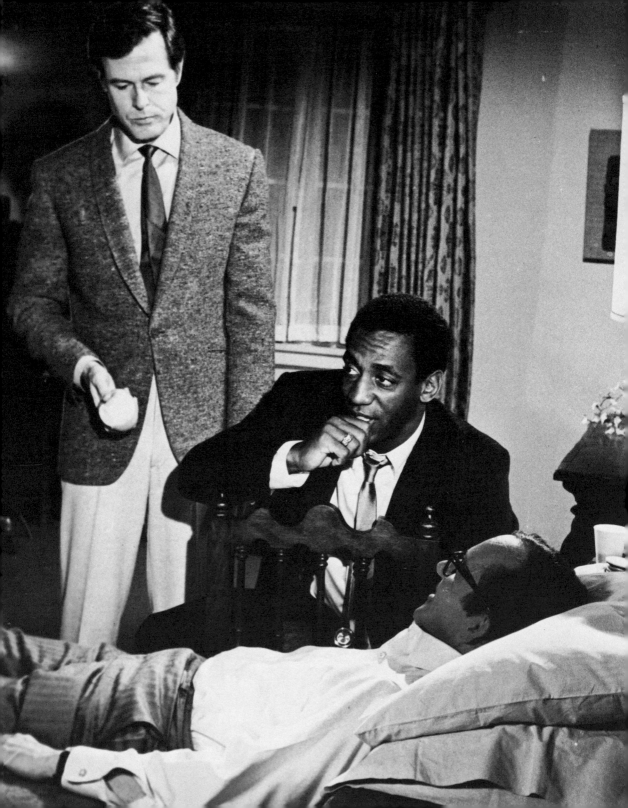

Bill's career in the early 1960s was becoming many-layered like a birthday cake. His role in a new television program, "I Spy," would make him a star. His co-star was Robert Culp, a white actor who, even today, is one of Bill's close friends.

"I Spy" was the first television series where a black and a white actor were treated as equals. Before this program blacks had been given less important— or supporting—roles on TV.

Bill Cosby and Robert Culp in a scene from their TV show "I Spy"

Culp and Cosby played spies who traveled the world pretending to be a coach and a tennis player. Their dangerous and funny adventures appealed to audiences.

"I Spy" was a hit. In 1966 Bill was honored by the National Academy of Television Arts and Sciences when he received the first of four Emmy awards. His face was familiar to millions of Americans.

On the strength of his success in "I Spy," Bill was offered his own TV show. From 1969 to 1971 on NBC's "Bill Cosby Show" he played a gym teacher. There followed a weekly CBS program and an ABC variety show for children.

When he was 28 years old, Bill won an Emmy Award for his role in "I Spy." He was the first black actor to win an Emmy for a leading role in a TV series.

Success was followed by praise and more success. Musicians honored Bill for his longtime interest in jazz by making him president of the Rhythm and Blues Hall of Fame. Bill also became a movie star. He appeared with Robert Culp in *Hickey and Boggs* and in *Uptown Saturday Night* and *Let's Do It Again* with fellow black actor and friend, Sidney Poitier. More than five other movie roles came his way during the 1970s.

Meanwhile, Bill decided to return to college. By 1977 he had earned a Ph.D. degree in education from the University of Massachusetts—meaning he could be called "Dr. Cosby." Eventually he was elected a trustee of Temple University, the school he had left to enter show business. He now felt that each person must take charge of developing his or her own mind.

Sidney Poitier and Bill Cosby in a scene from their movie *A Piece of the Action.* The two actors were a very popular comedy team.

Bill Cosby realized that children could learn while they were laughing. Characters he had created like Dumb Donald, Weird Harold, and Fat Albert became part of a popular TV cartoon series. The series, known as "Fat Albert and the Cosby Kids," is still being shown on television. Many of the cartoon scenes take place on the same kind of city streets Bill walked as a boy.

He also appeared on the award-winning "Electric Company" and "Sesame Street" programs. And, to help preschool children enjoy reading and writing, Bill made "Picture Pages" for a cable television channel.

Bill has appeared on numerous educational TV shows for children.

READ

Bill Cosby
and friends
for America's
Libraries

At home, Bill and his wife, Camille, talked to their children about drugs. They explained that drug abuse could destroy lives. Because Bill felt as many children as possible should hear the message, he recorded an album called *Bill Cosby Talks to Kids About Drugs*.

In the 1980s Bill has a lot to celebrate. Everyone sees him on TV commercials. These commercials, in addition to his live performances, movies, and TV appearances, have made him a millionaire many times over. He can afford many cars, an art collection, a private jet plane, and five houses. A favorite home is a farmhouse in Amherst, Massachusetts, which Camille has furnished with antique American furniture.

Bill believes strongly in the value
of education and the joy of reading.
He appeared in this poster celebrating
National Library Week.

But Bill Cosby has never forgotten what it is like to be poor. He and Camille give their money and time to help people of all races. Black causes receive their special attention. They work for The National Association of Sickle Cell Disease, Inc. (a disease that affects many black Americans) and for Operation PUSH, headed by the Reverend Jesse Jackson. In 1983 PUSH (People United to Serve Humanity) honored Bill by giving him the group's Frederick Douglass Memorial Premiere Award. Because Bill and Camille Cosby believe more blacks should vote and attend college and graduate school, they actively support organizations that help in these areas.

Bill Cosby at a fund-raising event for the Reverend Jesse Jackson's (seen right) Operation Push

Honors and awards keep coming to Bill. Universities like Harvard and Brown have granted him honorary degrees. In addition, the one-time high school dropout received a Lifetime Achievement in Comedy Award from a famous Harvard University magazine called the *Lampoon*.

Such a talented performer can no longer be called just a "comedian." Bill Cosby is an actor, an entertainer, and a teacher. He continues to stretch himself—to attempt new things. In 1983, with Sammy Davis, Jr., he appeared on stage at the Gershwin Theater in New York City in a show called *Two Friends. The New York Times* newspaper said, "Bill Cosby is at home on a Broadway stage . . . sending the audience into gales of laughter."

Bill Cosby carries TV actor Emmanuel Lewis as they arrive at the Apollo Theater in New York City, 1985. Cosby hosted a show to celebrate the reopening of the theater and its fiftieth anniversary.

Children continue to hold a special place in Bill Cosby's life—both his own and the millions who watch him on TV. "The Cosby Show" is filmed before a live audience, and sometimes one scene has to be done over many times until it is right. But Bill is patient with the show's young actors. "Bill is real honest, and he goes out of his way to help us," said Lisa Bonet in an interview with *People* magazine. She plays teenager Denise on the show.

A gentle teacher, Bill Cosby uses laughter to make his points. His audiences feel good about themselves.

"His show makes me feel like I want to watch it again," one nine-year-old says. Another child comments, "Bill teaches you things without your even realizing it."

In a scene from "The Cosby Show," Cliff playfully paddles Rudy (Keshia Knight Pulliam) while her sister Vanessa (Tempestt Bledsoe) referees the match.

People who laugh together, Bill believes, may be willing to work together. "Look, we're all facing the same problems," he points out.

Today's kids will have to deal with tough probiems when they become tomorrow's grownups. But his own life has taught Bill it's up to each person to make an effort. He says:

When you begin to choose something you want to do, you can enter areas you have never tried before. You can become successful, but first you must have some sort of feeling for it. How do you get a feeling for it? Sometimes the answer is "try." If you don't try, you will never know.

In a scene from "The Cosby Show," Cliff (Bill Cosby) proves to his children that they don't spend enough time thinking about Father's Day gifts by wearing his assortment of strange presents all at once.

INDEX